No Compromise

Abiding in the Glory of God

By Jo Ann Stinyard

Since 2009
Tallahassee • Plant City

Copyright © 2023 by Jo Ann Stinyard

All rights reserved. This book is protected under the copyright laws of the United States of America. This book may not be copied or reprinted for commercial gain or profit. No portion of this book may be reproduced, stored in a retrieval system, or transmitted in any form or by any means—electronic, mechanical, photocopy, recording, scanning, or other—without the prior written permission of the author. Brief quotations in critical reviews or articles are not permitted without the consent of the author. Permissions will be granted upon request.

ISBN-13: 978-1-7370620-9-7

Heart.Ink Press, LLC
www.heartinkpress.com
Tuned to the beat of your heart.
Manifesting dreams and visions.

Printed in the United States of America

Dedication

This book is dedicated to all who took the time to read From Confusion to the Knowledge of God and were ultimately blessed and encouraged to be the best born again Christian they could be all for the glory of God. It's also dedicated to all the Apostles, Prophets, Evangelist, Pastors, and Teachers who have ever poured into me and helped prepare me for my journey. I won't call everyone by name, but I must honor my leaders Bishop Joel Brown and Pastor Tiffanie Brown of Faith Celebration Church in Lakeland, Florida. You both are such loving, caring, and compassionate lovers of God and His people and I thank you for loving me well and equipping me for the work of the ministry.

Inspiration

Thank you to my Lord and Savior Jesus Christ for showing me who I am and who you are, and that apart from you I can do nothing.

John 15:5-8 (MSG), "I am the Vine; you are the branches. When you're joined with me and I with you, the relation intimate and organic, the harvest is sure to be abundant. Separated, you can't produce a thing. Anyone who separates from me is deadwood, gathered up and thrown on the bonfire. But if you make yourselves at home with me and my words are at home in you, you can be sure that whatever you ask will be listened to and acted upon. This is how my Father shows who he is—when you produce grapes, when you mature as my disciples."

Table of Contents

CHAPTER 1
In the Glory! — 9

CHAPTER 2
Where Am I Now? — 19

CHAPTER 3
Enrollment - Time to Enroll in Warfare Boot Camp — 31

CHAPTER 4
Standard Operating Procedures (SOP) — 35

CHAPTER 5
Let the Great Teacher Teach You! — 61

CHAPTER 6
Steps to Deliverance — 83

CHAPTER 7
Congratulations - Certificate of Completion — 95

Chapter 1
IN THE GLORY

It was the best decision of my life to surrender to the Lord Jesus Christ in 2005. The journey has been amazing, but it was a process to get to where I am now; "Abiding in the Glory of God."

For those of you who have read my first book, *From Confusion to the Knowledge of God*, I believe that without a doubt you were able to see the presence and power of God operating in my life. However, if you had asked me then "What is the glory of God?" I would not have been able to answer that question fully, completely, or thoroughly. So, for those of you who are saying to yourselves, "What does that mean?" Although difficult to define, I'm going to try to define it to the best of my ability (God's divine ability) and with the wisdom of multiple counselors in my life.

In Isaiah 6:1-3 (NIV), it says, "In the year that King Uzziah died, I saw the Lord, high and exalted, seated on a throne; and the train of his robe filled the temple. Above him were seraphim, each with six wings: With two wings they covered their faces, with two they covered their feet, and with two they were flying. And they were calling to one another:

'Holy, holy, holy is the LORD Almighty;
  the whole earth is full of his glory.'"

Isaiah said that he *saw*, which indicates that there was a manifested presence of God. Day and night God's creation is speaking forth His glory and as God's people we are glory carriers. Has anyone ever said to you, "I see God in you" or "Your face is glowing"? Moses displayed God's glory when he came down from the mount. The Bible says that his face was radiant, glowing, and shining and some translations say that his face sent forth beams. We as believers have the indwelling presence of God and because we are in His presence we can see and feel the weight of His glory; everything contained in the character of God, the grandest thing about Him. There is nothing like feeling the healing, the comfort, and the external splendor and majesty of His miracles, signs, and wonders. Especially when the people of God come together in unity to worship.

Therefore, the glory of God is not just what we see and feel, it's everything. It's the manifested presence of God and the public display of His infinite worth, power, and radiance. His beauty, external splendor, and majesty, His greatness and sovereignty. It's everything!

You may be saying, "How do you experience it?" Well, if you are a believer in the Lord Jesus Christ, it's built in and all you have to do is look for it, pray for it, prepare for it (because it's big) and walk in it.

So, was it easy to get to this place? Certainly not, but I found myself in a place of hunger and thirst for more of God, just as Moses was in Exodus 33. God was making a promise to Moses that His presence would go with him, but Moses wanted more, an assurance; a confidence that God's presence will be with him. I can imagine that it must have caused a little anxiety to be asked to do such a great thing as to lead the people out of Egypt. Just as it causes a little pause or unease when we clearly see what God is calling us to do. Getting a glimpse of your calling is mind blowing and you want to know that God is with you.

But, when the glory of God shows up, it causes all His goodness to pass in front of you.

Exodus 33:18-19 (NIV), "Then Moses said, 'Now show me your glory.' And the LORD said, 'I will cause all my goodness to pass in front of you, and I will proclaim my name, the LORD, in your presence. I will have mercy on whom I will have mercy, and I will have compassion on whom I will have compassion."

The Bible also records that we go from glory to glory, in 2 Corinthians 3:18. As we turn our hearts over to God and come to the knowledge that there is now no condemnation for those who are in Christ Jesus and take hold of the righteousness within us through the grace of Christ, we will be transformed little by little to reflect that inner glory. Hence, from glory to glory, being changed from the glory of the old to the glory of the new.

Great men and leaders in the Kingdom often say that greatness takes time. So, there was a lot of processing in my journey and there still is to this day. The best definition of the word *process* that I have found in order to make my statement clear is: a natural continuing action or series of actions or changes, the process of growth; life processes, mental processes, a series of actions or operations leading to a result. In the process there was a vetting, a weeding out of things that could no longer reside in my soul. The process was sometimes uncomfortable, there were times when I did not understand what was going on. There were ups and downs, relationships that had to end, bad habits or tendencies which were sometimes hard to let go but had to go. There were days of frustration, crying, venting to God, and asking for strength. Since we are battling from a place of victory and not for it, there were days when I felt on top of the world and days when I felt as if I was all over the place and going nowhere. Not realizing that in everything there is a lesson to be learned, wisdom and understanding was gained and would be tools that would catapult me into my destiny. I found myself longing to live in a place of purity. And by 2023, the world was longing to do what they wanted do, right is wrong and wrong is right. So, I was misunderstood and dealt with a lot of persecution. But thanks be to God who always causes us to triumph, and no weapon formed was able to prosper. And now living in the glory; a place of forgiveness, grace, mercy, and favor. He has healed me completely and I want you to experience the exact same thing. I need you to understand that God is not a respecter of persons. If He did it for me, I know He can do the same for you. The Bible says in Proverbs 3:5-6, "Trust in the LORD with all your heart, and lean not on your own understanding; In all your ways acknowledge Him, And He shall direct your paths."

His word is bond, and it shall not return void. God immediately inspired me to write a follow-up to let you know where I am now, what I am doing now, and how I maintained my deliverance. I knew I was having the unction in my spirit to write another book, but to be honest, at first, I had no idea what He wanted it to be about. When God blessed me to write, "From Confusion to the Knowledge of God", I knew He wanted me to share my testimony of the lifestyle I was living and finally coming to the knowledge of knowing Him. But what's next? All you have to do is ask. He had four Prophets share with me the word of the Lord concerning book two. He also had a very good friend ask me a very important question. "So, I'm free, now how do I stay free?" Wow, now I had to write my formula out. What did I do, and how did I stay free?

Prayer: Father, I need you, please give me the wisdom on how to document my experience to help your people stay free. And allow me to stay, live, and abide always in this freedom you've given me. Lord, I don't want this book to be only for those dealing with sexual brokenness, but for all those struggling with any proclivity. You can deliver anyone from anything. You have my heart, now take my hands, and use them for your glory. In Jesus's name. Amen.

Chapter 2
WHERE AND HOW AM I NOW?

Free and staying free. Walking in the glory!

As of today, life has been amazing. The Lord has exceeded and continues to exceed my expectations. As my first book continues to bless those who would read it and those who would read it continue to share it, I can say with confidence that my first book was a divine download from God. I was told on numerous occasions by the readers that they could not put it down once they began to read. I was told that even though the person never had a homosexual proclivity, the book was still a huge blessing to those dealing with any type of unclean spirit. It caused their endurance to increase, knowing that God is with them. It caused their faith to increase for other family members dealing with identity issues. Some said the book was encouraging, inspirational, liberating and motivating. I was and am extremely humbled and blessed by the reviews. I was even more humbled by the fact that the readers said that they needed more and wanted to know how I am doing now.

It is now 2023, am I perfect, certainly not! But I am still free of sexual sins and identity issues. I will call them out so that you are clear. Homosexuality – FREE, Pornography – FREE, Masturbation – FREE, Transgenderism and Gender Dysphoria – FREE. I will also call out those things that are still a daily battle and process. We as believers must make it a priority in our lives to live holy, for He is holy; to be that living sacrifice, holy and acceptable to God which is our reasonable service. We must stay in a state of starving the flesh and feeding the spirit. Saints, listen carefully, pride is a pit, quicksand, and it goes before the fall. I say this because this is still a battle for me, there are days when pride will subtly sneak up on me. Most of the time, I am aware of it and immediately I rebuke it and repent. There are times when God must literally have a sit down with me. And I thank Him for those sit downs because this means He greatly cares about me, and He doesn't want to resist me. God resist the proud but gives grace to the humble (James 4:6-7). I would implore you, if you struggle with pride (and we all do at some point in our lives), to submit yourselves to God resist the devil and he will flee from you. Know that pride sometimes comes down from generation to generation. And Study to show yourself approved. This could be another book, but here is just a snippet. Leviathan is the king of pride, Job 41:1-34, pride has many children. Just to name a few, pride likes to group with: guilt, shame, condemnation, impatience, disobedience, complaining, gossiping and arrogance, self-righteousness, self-gratification, self-seduction, and self-will. And remember demonic spirits travel in groups, teams, and legions - 3,000-6000. So, study, study, study. This book is mostly about practical ways I was able to maintain my deliverance. Studying God's word and scriptural books that the Holy Spirit led me to has definitely been prominent.

I now live in a place of NO COMPROMISE, and I make this public declaration: Because I know who I am in Christ Jesus, I will not compromise my relationship with Him. I confess my faithfulness to my God, who has the name above all names. I have new standards! I am royalty according to 1 Peter 2:9, and there are just some things that royalty does not participate in. I will not fornicate or commit any other type of sexual immorality: homosexuality, masturbation, pornography. I rebuke any form of an unnatural act and confusion of the mind. I will not lie, steal, curse, walk in willful disobedience to the word of God and what He tells me to do. I will not hold bitterness or unforgiveness in my heart, I will not retaliate because vengeance belongs to God. I will not watch ungodly movies; I will not go places contrary to my standards just to please family or friends. I will not drink, smoke, or eat things just to please family or friends. I will not be conformed to this world, but I will be transformed by the renewing of my mind that I might prove what is the good, and perfect will of God for my life.

How is my family doing?

The Bible says in Romans 4:17 (NIV), "as it is written, 'I have made you a father of many nations. He is our father in the sight of God, in whom he believed—the God who gives life to the dead and calls into being things that were not."

I am calling it into being, pulling it from eternity. The God of eternity wrote our story before the foundations of the world. Before He formed us in our mother's womb, He knew us. So, I decree and declare: That my whole family is saved and walking with God, in perfect health and abundance. They are the head and not the tail, above only and not beneath, lenders and not borrowers. They walk in the fruit of the spirit: love, joy, peace, longsuffering, faithfulness, goodness, kindness, gentleness, and self-control. Every generational and ancestral curse that has come down our bloodline has been eradicated by the presence and power of God. In Jesus's name. Every root of bitterness and unforgiveness has been uprooted and every spirit of pride, manipulation, control, witchcraft, divination, occult involvement, ungodly soul ties and immoral relationships, lust, perversion, immorality, uncleanness, hatred, anger, resentment, revenge, retaliation and or addictions has been destroyed by the blood of Jesus. The blood of Jesus has washed, sanctified, and purified everyone in my family. And we walk in the newness of God. And it is so! In Jesus's name!

How is my health going?

One word, *astonishing* - extremely surprising or impressive, amazing.

I thank God for the leaders, prophets, and teachers that God has placed in my life. I realize that in this season, the enemy might try to find an open door through deception, weariness, distractions, and busyness. However, even though he might find a little crack to sneak into and it just so happens to get pass me, he will not get pass the prophets, leaders, and teachers in my life. That's why community and connection are so important. Whatever the enemy tries, it will be exposed. I know this for a fact. I experienced a season when the enemy was trying to use guilt, condemnation, insecurity, and pride to cause me to experience symptoms that I know had been destroyed by the blood of Jesus. The weapon formed did not prosper because the prophet in my life exposed all of it. I immediately broke off all agreement with any consequences of my past. I am blood bought, old things have passed away, all things have become new. As soon as I made a conscience decision to walk in the newness of God, then my help came, and my liberty arose. So having said that, ultimately, I feel amazing. I feel completely confident that I am healed by His stripes. And we all know, when you are a believer and you are actively doing the work of the ministry, soul winning, ministering inner healing to the broken hearted, bringing revelation to captive mines...you are a direct target to the enemy. He gets angry when we snatch a soul from the kingdom of darkness. Luke 4:13 says, "And when the devil had ended every temptation, he departed from him for a season."

He may depart for a season, but I must without a doubt stay diligent in balancing my life and getting proper rest, eating right and not letting the word of God depart from my mouth, and mediating therein day and night.

The enemy tries to tempt me to speak against my healing when I feel a familiar symptom. But he is defeated because as soon as I feel a symptom, I speak the truth, the word of God. Even though I feel one way, I thank God that I am healed, that according to His word in Psalms 103:3, that he forgives all our iniquities and heals all our diseases. I thank God as I read His word, it is healing to my flesh (Proverbs 4:20-23). What are the doctors saying? Rheumatologist, "blood work is good and stable." Hematologist, "What have you been doing? Whatever you have been doing continue to do it." Nephrologist, "Amazing, you used to have an extreme amount of protein in your urine (2000 milligrams) which could be a sign of kidney disease, now you have 200 milligrams and less than 150 is normal." I am claiming that in my next visit in 6 months, I will be normal, in Jesus's name.

So, as you can see, deliverance is a process in some areas, but there are some areas that I have mastered, through God's grace, teachings, and revelations. In the areas that I have mastered, my desire more than anything in this world is to help others to be free, so they also can help others; hence, disciples are multiplied. When I talked about my doctors and their specialties, I did that on purpose to make this point. If I was dealing with a blood disorder caused by Lupus, then I would need to see a specialist in that area. What am I saying? Things that used to be my mess, are now my ministry and I specialize in certain things. Just as you specialize in certain things that God has brought you out of. My prayer for you is that you walk in your calling.

I am currently the founder of Grace-In-Motion Ministries Inc., which is a non-for-profit organism (note: living organism) where our focus is to minister the love of Christ to those dealing with sexual brokenness. This blessed organism is also modeled after James 1:27, pure and undefiled religion, seeing about those who are often forgotten about: widows, orphans, homeless, veterans, prisons, domestic violence shelters, visual impaired, quadriplegic, mental disorders. Question: when is the last time you assisted somebody with these challenges? I will leave that right there, for you to marinate in.

Being a believer, who worked in Law Enforcement for 20 years, I met various people from various cultures, I have experienced and seen so many things and I have been able to minister to people through various crises in their lives. I did not see all this or experience all this for no reason. God is using what I saw and learned throughout the years. This is why Grace-In-Motion has a primary focus with no limits to whom can be touched by the ministry. I love the Lord and I love people.

Chapter 3
ENROLLMENT - TIME TO ENROLL IN WARFARE BOOTCAMP

Welcome to Abiding in the Glory Boot Camp!

Congratulations on taking the first step in reaching your spiritual goals. It is my prayer that your life will never be the same and that you will become amazingly and supernaturally whole. I pray supernatural increase, greatness, and newness upon you. I pray for a divine ability to understand His words on a level that would exceed your expectations.

When I enrolled in the Police Academy and took my first job with Clearwater Police Department, there was an entire ceremony where you took the oath that went something like this:

"On my honor, I will never betray my integrity, my character or the public trust. I will always have the courage to hold myself and others accountable for our actions. I will always maintain the highest ethical standards and uphold the values of my community, and the agency I serve."

Great words huh? However, I am no longer a police officer, I traded in my uniform for the Armor of God, and you and I are now enlisted in the Army of God through our faith in Jesus Christ. So, we are going to make our own declarations:

We Declare: It is an honor and privilege to serve our God who loved us so much that He gave his only begotten son. Our God who humbled Himself and became obedient to the point of death, even the death of the cross.

There is nothing we can do to repay Him for His great sacrifice; however, it is our ambition to please Him. We will do what He requires of us, which is to do good, love mercy, and walk humbly before our God. We will make it paramount to "love the LORD our God with all our heart, with all our soul, and with all our mind. Which is the first and greatest commandment. And *the* second *is* like it: We will love our neighbor as ourselves" (Matthew 22:37-39).

We decree and declare that the God we serve (Jesus) Jehovah Gibbor (The Mighty God), will be with us in trouble, will deliver us and honor us and with long life, will satisfy us and show us His salvation. In Jesus's name.

Without further ado, LET'S GO!

Chapter 4
STANDARD OPERATING PROCEDURES (SOP)

What did I do? How did I maintain my deliverance?

The first step is total surrender. What is surrender? Surrender – to give oneself up into the power of another, especially as a prisoner. It is no longer about you; you belong to God. Biblically, Paul the Apostle in Ephesians 4:1 called himself a prisoner for the Lord and urged us to live a life worthy of the calling we have received. This is a complete dying to self. Paul said in Galatians 2:20, "I have been crucified with Christ; it is no longer I who live, but Christ lives in me, and the life which I now live in the flesh I live in the Son of God, who loved me and gave Himself for me." The Lord gave Himself for us and now we are giving ourselves to Him.

Vision: When I hear the word surrender, I always think of the vision God gave me concerning surrender. In this vision, I saw myself in my police uniform chasing a suspect. The chase went on and on through many obstacles, barriers, hurdles, and stumbling blocks like fences and backyards with pit bulls that were ready to bite, and different forms of surfaces, wet slippery roads, grass, and rocks. As the pursuit was coming to an end, I saw that the suspect was becoming weary. And in that weariness, the suspect finally drops to his knees and places his hands up in the air.

The suspect was tired. When you come to a place of surrendering to God, you have tried everything else, you have been through every obstacle or stumbling block, and you are tired of being sick and tired. Surrendering is the key to your freedom. Once you do this, it will be easier to receive everything a life in Christ has to offer.

The second step is to ask the Lord to come into your life. Simple words from your heart: God, I need you. I admit that I am a sinner. I believe that you died for my sins and rose again on the third day. I ask you to come into my life and be my Lord and Savior. I turn my back on sin and reach out to you that I might receive eternal life.

<u>Scriptures to know and commit to memory:</u>

John 3:16, "For God so loved the world that He gave His only begotten Son, that whoever believes in Him should not perish but have everlasting life."

Romans 5:8, "But God demonstrates His own love toward us, in that while we were still sinners, Christ died for us."

Romans 10:9 (NKJV), "that if you confess with your mouth the Lord Jesus and believe in your heart that God has raised Him from the dead, you will be saved."

Romans 10:13 (NKJV), "For 'whoever calls on the name of the Lord shall be saved.'"

Hebrews 10:12, "But this Man, after He had offered one sacrifice for sins forever, sat down at the right hand of God."

The third step is to Find a good Bible-based church. What am I saying? You are now a Christian – a believer in Christ. So, you want a church that teaches Christian doctrine, beliefs. Your objective it to learn and grow in your relationship with Christ. Keep in mind that there is no perfect church, simply because we are there and it's for imperfect people. It is like a hospital.

My Story: After my encounter with the Lord Jesus in my little 1-bedroom apartment, I knew I needed community and connection with those who were walking with and building a relationship with Christ. It's like when I was attending the Police Academy, it becomes like a small family and our goal was the same, to become a police officer. We helped each other study, develop connections with those already in law enforcement, and when we needed to talk or vent about our day, we were there for each other. The church is just that, a family, community, a place of divine connections.

Being that I was coming out of homosexuality, a lifestyle that was considered taboo and unfortunately many people, even leaders, did not know how to relate nor what to do and they experienced a little discomfort ministering to those who have been in that lifestyle. Sadly, some even had a different level of dislike or prejudice when it came to the

LGBTQIA community even if they were delivered. And at the time, I was saved, delivered and on fire for God. The transformation was happening on the inside of me, but the outside exterior, the way I looked and dressed still needed to be worked on, the process was just beginning. I knew I needed a place where there was a level of comfortability. Such as people who didn't look at the exterior of a person and pass judgment and letting that interrupt the beauty of developing awesome relationships with different people with different backgrounds.

So, I called up my spiritual brother and gave him the good news, "I'm saved, and I need a church." He knew my situation, so he immediately went into action. He set up a meeting with a Pastor that loved people (period) and had a few members that had come out of the homosexual lifestyle. The connection was just what I needed. I grew and I grew with my relationship with Christ.

In my growing, I realized that I was hungry for as much training as I could get. Remember, I was para-military, so I loved training. Every believer needs a place where they can grow. And after a long journey, God transitioned me and led me to that very place (and God also will lead you to the right place), Faith Celebration Church in Lakeland, Florida, under the leadership of Bishop Joel Brown and Pastor Tiffanie Brown. FCC embodies the goal of the church, which is explained in Ephesians 4:11-13 (NLT), "Now these are the gifts Christ gave to the church: the apostles, the prophets, the evangelists, and the pastors and teachers. Their responsibility is to equip God's people to do his work and build up the church, the body of Christ. This will continue until we all come to such unity in our faith and knowledge of God's Son that we will be mature in the Lord, measuring up to the full and complete standard of Christ."

I realized that this is the type of church I needed to equip me to do the work and ministry that God had placed in me.

1) A church with a new members class. This is where you find out if they are teaching Christian doctrine and you learn the structure, mission and vision of the ministry.

2) Immediate discipleship classes. Notice I said immediate. Jesus immediately taught and modeled for His disciples; He wanted them to reach their full potential so they could disciple others. Hence, the great commission. Matthew 28:19-20, "Go therefore and make disciples of all the nations, baptizing them in the name of the Father and of the Son and of the Holy Spirit, teaching them to observe all things that I have commanded you; and lo, I am with you always, *even* to the end of the age." Amen.

3) A church that implements accountability partners or small groups giving you an opportunity to share, grow, and teach others the things the Holy Spirit has revealed and taught you. Leadership is not always available to assist or pray for you all the time. So having an accountability partner is very helpful.

4) A church that has prayer times during the day and at night, and teachings about prayer along with the Bible studies and Sunday services. Prayer is key and vital to your relationship with the Lord. If you become a great prayer warrior or intercessor, you will be highly in tune with the voice of God.

5) Training courses on the teachings of Jesus, the Holy Spirit, faith, evangelism, identifying the enemy, prophetic training and how to identify and function in your spiritual giftings, management and finance, and teaching you stewardship. God's plan for your

finances as well as equipping leaders to make good financial decisions for yourself and the church.

Note: All churches may not be equipped to instruct on all these things. As you grow, you will come to identify exactly what you need for your equipping. If you are attending a church that does not offer all the things that you need, it does not necessarily mean you must leave. Remember, you have the Holy Spirit that will guide you along. You may have to seek out a good Bible school or college along your equipping journey. There are many courses offered online. Since I chose an Apostolic/Prophetic church, Ephesians 4:11, I needed Apostolic/Prophetic teachings. I have some extraordinary leaders and I can say that I am becoming more and more equipped to do the work of the ministry. I thank God that I have found great leaders to teach me in areas that I was lacking in.

The fourth step is to learn how to be battle ready. Get well dressed, suited up!

I will be perfectly honest with you in my journey, the Holy Spirit led me to many spiritual warfare materials that are in my arsenal till this day. I believe knowing who you are fighting, what you are fighting for, and how to fight is vital to your walk. Early on I knew I was fighting a very crafty devil and his cohorts. Even the more, I know the devil knows the scriptures which made him more deceptive in his tactics. I have never been in the military, but I have read books written by born again believers who were in the military that were very powerful. Since they were soldiers, they were well trained, they knew their enemy and they knew their plan of battle. We as believers need to be battle ready. The Lord is so faithful, and He speaks *Jo Ann* to me. What am I saying? He speaks my language so I can relate to and understand Him. He will meet you right where you're at. So being that I was a Police Officer, the Lord ministered Ephesians 6:10-19 to me in such a way that I was able to relate it to my uniform. Somewhat like Paul, he used the Roman Soldier that was guarding him in prison as an example to believers of how they should put on their spiritual armor.

God promises us that He will never leave us or forsake us in Hebrews 13:5! He is our refuge and our fortress. He is our protection according to Psalms 91. Even though we have an enemy that is fighting against us daily, God is so faithful that He gives us the weapons to fight with. God gave us a very powerful weapon that many of us tend to overlook. That weapon is the Armor of God: "finally, my brethren, be strong in the lord and in the power of his might. put on the whole armor of God, that you may be able to stand against the wiles of the devil." Ephesians 6:10-11, this is a spiritual armor that Paul speaks about that believers ought to be sure to put on daily. He wrote the book of Ephesians while he was in prison. He was unjustly placed into prison for preaching the gospel of Jesus Christ. He used the Roman soldier that was watching over him as an example to believers of how they should put on their armor to battle against the devil. Historically, the Roman soldiers put on their armor to fight battles against their enemies. In Ephesians 6:14, Paul said to have your waist girded with truth. He used the Roman soldier's belt that hung around his waist. This is where all of the weapons were.

Since the devil is a liar, when you walk in truth, you're walking in integrity. One of the seven things that the Lord hates is a lying tongue (Proverbs 6:16-19). Verse 14 (Ephesians 6) says to put on the breastplate of righteousness - *righteousness* is purity. The breastplate of the Roman soldier covered his vital organs. Righteousness covers us and keeps us from the lust of the eyes, the lust of the flesh, and the pride of life. Verse 15, "having your feet shod with the preparation of the gospel of peace." *Peace* is tranquility, you will have peace in the midst of your storms. Remember, Jesus went to sleep on the boat and there was a tremendous storm going on (Mark 4:38-40).

Verse 16, "above all, taking the shield of faith, with which you will be able to quench all the fiery darts of the enemy." *Faith* is certainty, faith says God is your deliverer and your keeper. If the fiery darts of the enemy get in, it could cause doubt, unbelief, confusion, and the like.

Verse 17, "and take the helmet of salvation, the helmet of salvation covers your thoughts and keeps them pure." Free from depression, anxiety, fear, and the torment of suicidal thoughts. It's the helmet of sanity. Verse 17 goes on to say, "and the sword of the spirit, which is the word of God. the word of God is the way the truth and the life." We should read the word of God daily. God's word will not return void. Literally the word will speak to you, keep you, and be a lamp to your feet and a light to your path (Psalms 119:105). I encourage you to put on your spiritual armor daily. It is our defense.

Who are we fighting?

We should know who our enemy is! Ephesians 6:12 says, "for we do not wrestle against flesh and blood, but against principalities, against powers, against the rulers of the darkness of this age, against spiritual *hosts* of wickedness in the heavenly *places*."

So now we have to recognize that it's not our boss on the job, it's not our president, judicial system, economic system or our families that we are fighting against.

What are we fighting for?

Let this encourage you, we are fighting from victory not for victory. Jesus took care of that part. We can't lose since He took victory in His hands and now sits at the right hand of God. However, we still have to fight to maintain our deliverance to get everything the Lord has for us on this side of heaven and receive our crowns, glory to God, "We shall wear a crown."

Some people think that there is no work to do after salvation is received. Not so. I'll give you an example: If you buy a new car, it's nice, it smells new, it affordable, it gets great gas mileage, but if you don't take care of it, you will break down on the interstate just like when you had your old hooptie. Your new car requires maintenance. Listen carefully, your spiritual life and relationship with the Lord Jesus requires maintenance. Get your oil changes, rotate your tires, and wash and clean your car. Ok, for some of you, it still didn't click, it's ok, that's why we have the Holy Spirit. Get your oil changed. Isaiah 43:18-19, "Do not remember the former things, nor consider the things of old. Behold, I will do a new thing, now it shall spring forth;

Shall you not know it? I will even make a road in the wilderness, *And* rivers in the desert." He tells us to let the old go, because you can't put new wine into old wine skin. Forgive, maximize the moment, and forward march soldier. Rotate your tires. The physical tires on your car need to be kept in good condition or they will go flat. Don't go flat. 2 Peter 1:5-8 says, "but also for this very reason, giving all diligence, add to your faith virtue, to virtue knowledge, to knowledge self-control, to self-control perseverance, to perseverance godliness, to godliness brotherly kindness, and to brotherly kindness love. For if these things are yours and abound, *you* will be neither barren nor unfruitful in the knowledge of our Lord Jesus Christ." James 1:2-4 says, "brethren, count it all joy when you fall into various trials, knowing that the testing of your faith produces patience. But let patience have *its* perfect work, that you may be perfect and complete, lacking nothing."

Lastly, 2 Peter 3:18 says, "but grow in the grace and knowledge of our Lord and Savior Jesus Christ. To Him *be* the glory both now and forever. Amen." Wash and clean your car. Psalms 51:1-2 says, "have mercy upon me, O God, According to Your loving kindness; According to the multitude of Your tender mercies, Blot out my transgressions. Wash me thoroughly from my iniquity, and cleanse me from my sin."

Ok, I see you taking a praise break. We're moving forward. We can't turn back, say this with me, "I refuse to turn back." Hebrews 10:38, "Now the just shall live by faith; But if *anyone* draws back, my soul has no pleasure in him." We want to hear the words, "Well done, my good and faithful servant, you have been faithful over a few things, I will make you ruler of many, enter into the joy of the Lord" (Matthew 25:21).

The fifth step is to learn, maintain, and be consistent with these important practical everyday things.

1. Reading God's Word (take your medication, this is your lifeline)

Whenever I feel weak, find myself worrying, disappointed, discouraged or confused about how things turn out, I always remind myself that it was the word of God that brought me out of bondage. Proverbs 11:9 says, "the hypocrite with *his* mouth destroys his neighbor, but through knowledge the righteous will be delivered." I read 1 Corinthians 6:9-11, Romans 1:24-28, Leviticus 18:22, and 1 Timothy 1:8-1. When this knowledge went inside my eye gate and into my spirit, it became Rhema – living and active. It transformed my life.

2. Renew your mind. Romans 12:1-2 says, "I beseech you therefore, brethren, by the mercies of God, that you present your bodies a living

sacrifice, holy, acceptable to God, *which is* your reasonable service. And do not be conformed to this world, but be transformed by the renewing of your mind, that you may prove what *is* that good and acceptable and perfect will of God."

The word "renewing" in this verse was translated from the Greek word *ANAKAINOSIS*, and this word means "renovation" (Strong's Concordance). We don't just need to remove walls and redo wiring over our natural minds; we need a total renovation. Many of us think that if we are good at fulfilling the conditions of Romans 12:1, then everything else would automatically work out. However, Paul went on to state that we also have to renew our minds. Many of us have made a genuine commitment to the Lord but haven't renewed our minds through God's word and have only found ourselves needlessly going through difficulties in many areas of our lives.

3. Meditate on God's Word.

The benefits of meditating on God's word!

    A. It's wise. Proverbs 1:7 says, "the fear of the LORD *is* the beginning of knowledge, *But* fools despise wisdom and instruction."

    B. It increases faith and trust in God. Hebrews 10:38 says, "Now the just shall live by faith", Proverbs 3:5-6 says, "Trust in the LORD with all your heart, and lean not on your own understanding; In all your ways acknowledge Him, and He shall direct your paths."

    C. It casts down arguments. 2 Corinthians 10:4-6 says, "For the weapons of our warfare *are* not carnal but mighty in God for pulling down strongholds, casting down arguments and every high thing that exalts itself against the knowledge of God, bringing every thought into captivity to the obedience of Christ, and being ready to punish all disobedience when your obedience is fulfilled." Repetition is key to safety in what God said because He is not a man that He should lie nor the son of man that He should repent.

4. Do the Word (apply the word). James 1:22 says, "but be doers of the word, and not hearers only, deceiving yourselves. For if anyone is a hearer of the word and not a doer, he is like a man observing his natural face in a mirror." Joshua 1:8 says, "This Book of the Law shall not depart from your mouth, but you shall meditate in it day and night, that you may observe to do according to all

that is written in it. For then you will make your way prosperous, and then you will have good success."

5. Develop an attitude of thanksgiving. Sometimes its arm-twisting to be thankful when all hell is breaking loose, but as I was saying earlier, God has placed a lot of great people around me in this season of my life. And a good friend, leader, minister of the gospel, Dr. Lexus Potts, wrote a devotional entitled "The Journey to Gratitude." She made a powerful statement that jumped off the page, "There is something good in the midst of the bad, we just have to pause and look for it!" Wow powerful! And now, even though hard to do, I thank God no matter the circumstance.

David said in Psalms 34, "I will bless the LORD at all times; His praise *shall* continually *be* in my mouth. My soul shall make its boast in the LORD; The humble shall hear *of it* and be glad. Oh, magnify the LORD with me, And let us exalt His name together."

Death in the family, I will bless the Lord. Kids acting up, I will bless the Lord. Loss of my job, I will bless the Lord. Bad doctor's report, I will bless the Lord. House in foreclosure, I will bless the Lord. Car repossessed; I will bless the Lord. Grateful and Thankful in all circumstances. 1 Thessalonians 5:18 (ESV), "give thanks in all circumstances; for this is the will of God in Christ Jesus for you."

6. Develop a seriousness about staying free. When you are serious about something it means it is of great importance, worthy of attention, and is noteworthy in your life.

Paul said in Romans 6:1-4 (NKJV), "What shall we say then? Shall we continue in sin that grace may abound? Certainly not! How shall we who died to sin live any longer in it? Or do you not know that as many of us as were baptized into Christ Jesus were baptized into His death? Therefore, we were buried with Him through baptism into death, that just as Christ was raised from the dead by the glory of the Father, even so we also should walk in newness of life." We are new and dead to sin, so let us be serious and continually reckon to stay new and dead to sin.

Chapter 5
LET THE GREAT TEACHER TEACH YOU!

John 14:26 (NIV), "But the Advocate, the Holy Spirit, whom the Father will send in my name, will teach you all things and will remind you of everything I have said to you."

In this chapter, let us be intentional about listening to the Holy Spirit as He teaches, uses my experiences, and reminds us of who we are and how we must conduct ourselves in this world we live in. We are in this world, but we are not of this world.

Now that you are saved and developing in your walk with Christ, I want to give a strong caution to you. Being saved doesn't mean being perfect! You are a spiritual being, who lives in a body, and you possess a soul. This body we live in, the flesh, there is no good thing that dwells there. Let me be clearer, Paul in the book of Romans explained this fight with the flesh, let's take a look at the text in different translations for clarity.

Romans 7:15-20 (NKJV), "For what I am doing, I do not understand. For what I will to do, that I do not practice; but what I hate, that I do. If, then, I do what I will not to do, I agree with the law that it is good. But now, it is no longer I who do it, but sin that dwells in me. For I know that in me (*that is, in my flesh*) nothing good dwells; for to will is present with me, but how to perform what is good I do not find. For the good that I will to do, I do not do; but the evil I will not to do, that I practice. Now if I do what I will not to do, it is no longer I who do it, but sin that dwells in me."

Romans 7:15-20 (NLT), "I don't really understand myself, for I want to do what is right, but I don't do it.

Instead, I do what I hate. But if I know that what I am doing is wrong, this shows that I agree that the law is good. So, I am not the one doing wrong; it is sin living in me that does it. And I know that nothing good lives in me, that is, in my sinful nature. I want to do what is right, but I can't. I want to do what is good, but I don't. I don't want to do what is wrong, but I do it anyway. But if I do what I don't want to do, I am not really the one doing wrong; it is sin living in me that does it."

I wanted you to see this text in the NLT to bring more clarity. Paul was going through some push and pull in his flesh. He wanted to do what was right, but he did what was wrong anyway. My God, I can relate to that. What about you?

I could remember in just the first month of my salvation in 2005, having this struggle. The flesh has a mind of its own and it will cry out for what it was used to. For 33 years, I had given my flesh exactly what it wanted. Now, I wanted to walk in the spirit and not fulfill the lust of the flesh.

But being that I was a novice, saved but not really or fully understanding spiritual things, I was still trying to do things in the physical (or natural). I thought in my first couple of months, there was no other work to be done. "I'm saved. I got this." I'm not turning back to my sinful ways. "Oh, but the Flesh!"

If you read my first book, you know I'm an open book. However, the Holy Spirit prompted me to expound on chapter 8. And to let you know that I did in fact take a fall in my first few months of salvation. Jesus did in fact, step in and save me. However, He had to teach me how to fast and pray, and He gave me knowledge, understanding, and wisdom on the dos and don'ts.

So here is the story. After I got saved, all I wanted was to immediately tell others about Jesus Christ, I was like the woman at the well, who dropped her water pot, yelling "Come see a Man." I wanted everyone to receive Jesus, to feel this amazing feeling of protection, joy, and peace. But not everybody was ready. I thought I could still hang out, love, and draw those who were still living a homosexual lifestyle. Maybe one day, but not while I was being purged, trained, taught, and mentored by the Holy Spirit. I needed to be approved. For example, at my job at the Police Department, you were considered a rookie for about 5-7 years; one friend that I had called me a rookie all the way to my 10th year. However, they say to feel comfortable and knowledgeable it takes an officer 5-7 years. So, look at me 3 months in trying to step out there with no training.

I thought I was strong enough to have an old friend around me, even old girlfriends. I had to learn and what I learned is that when you don't acknowledge how strong your flesh can be, you will end up messing up, hindering your growth process, and grieving God.

It reminds me of Genesis 6:6 (NLT), "So the LORD was sorry he had ever made them and put them on the earth. It broke his heart." And one of the most excruciating pains, is to feel like you broke God's heart.

Yes, the Bible tells us in 1 John 1:9 (NKJV), "If we confess our sins, He is faithful and just to forgive us *our* sins and to cleanse us from all unrighteousness."

But I took my fall really hard. I had thoughts like, "Am I really saved?" and "Why would I hurt God? He did all that for me and I went back." So, now I had to deal with guilt. But, my loving, forgiving, compassionate God walked me through all of it with patience.

Getting back to the story, I messed up and had my last sexual encounter with an old girlfriend 3 months into my salvation process. This particular girlfriend was one I could not shake. Even though I had other relationships, somehow, she could show up on the scene and the sex would always start back up like we never stopped.

This is why allowing the Holy Spirit to teach and train you on different things is vital. In this case, to teach you about SOUL TIES. I wrote that in caps because that is a homework assignment for you. That could be another book all by itself. This goes for individuals of all sexual preferences, those who have a promiscuous lifestyle. Public Service Announcement! You are joining souls with everyone you sleep with.

Genesis 2:24 (NKJV) says, "Therefore, a man shall leave his father and mother and be joined to his wife, and they shall become one flesh."

Matthew 19:4 (NKJV) says, "And He answered and said to them, 'Have you not read that He who made *them* at the beginning 'made them male and female,' and said, 'For this reason a man shall leave his father and mother and be joined to his wife, and the two shall become one flesh'? So then, they are no longer two but one flesh. Therefore, what God has joined together, let not man separate.'"

In this case, the devil likes to pervert everything God does, so even though God did not purpose for two women or two men to be joined, you still caused a soul tie because that was God's original intent for sexual experiences.

So, she called just to talk, hang out, etc. I thought I was strong enough; I'm saved and going to be a world renown evangelist and preacher. Nothing is going to stop me. So, she came over, we talked about my deliverance, and she actually said that she knew it would happen and she congratulated me. But before I knew it, we were rolling around on the floor, kissing, humping, and trash talking; you know what I'm talking about. However, this time it was a little different. There was a small still voice saying, "you are a preacher, a child of God." I immediately looked up, got up, and said, "I can't do this. I'm a preacher." So, things didn't go as far as they usually did, but to me it went far enough. I was devastated. This is when the training came. He taught me about my flesh, soul ties, and fasting. I enlisted into a 12-month course with the Holy Spirit. And as you see in Chapter 8, pg. 111 in my first book, God made a way of escape, and I wasn't chewed up and spit out by the devil.

So, how do I triumph over this longing in my flesh? The word of God! The scriptures tell us in Hebrews 4:11-13, that the word discovers our condition. "Let us therefore be diligent to enter that rest, lest anyone fall according to the same example of disobedience. For the word of God *is* living and powerful, and sharper than any two-edged sword, piercing even to the division of soul and spirit, and of joints and marrow, and is a discerner of the thoughts and intents of the heart. And there is no creature hidden from His sight, but all things *are* naked and open to the eyes of Him to whom we *must give* account."

So, even though I was saved, I had to go through the process of being purged – to rid myself of an unwanted quality, condition, or feelings.

From the inside out. The process starts on the inside. The heart, inner healing.

I really loved my God who first loved me, I wanted to live in the will of God with all my heart, but there were still these thoughts of wanting to do some things I used to do. Such as watching pornography which leads to masturbation. Then thoughts like, "Are you really saved?" and "Why are you thinking about such things, when you have a holy God who now lives in you?"

The truth of the matter is there are three things working against you: the world, the devil, and the flesh. Literally, you work against you.

Therefore, I truly realized that I was indeed in a serious spiritual battle and my most effective weapon of warfare was the word of God. So, I needed to arm myself daily, just as I put on my gun belt in the morning to go out to face only God knew what on the city streets of Tampa, I had to arm myself with the Word of God morning, noon, and night and actively praying and meditate on the scriptures throughout the day. For those of you who have enlisted into the army or the Police Academy, no one tells you, "Oh this is going to be easy", so we must definitely not think that the devil that had you bound for years is simply going to let you go without a fight. His sole purpose is to steal, kill, and destroy you, but Jesus came that we might have life and have it more abundantly (John 10:10).

Here are some weapons for the flesh:

Galatians 5:16-18 (NKJV), "I say then: Walk in the Spirit, and you shall not fulfill the lust of the flesh. For the flesh lusts against the Spirit, and the Spirit against the flesh; and these are contrary to one another, so that you do not do the things that you wish. But if you are led by the Spirit, you are not under the law."

Romans 8:6 (NKJV), "For to be carnally minded *is* death, but to be spiritually minded *is* life and peace."

1 Corinthians 10:13 (NKJV), "No temptation has overtaken you except such as is common to man; but God *is* faithful, who will not allow you to be tempted beyond what you are able, but with the temptation will also make the way of escape, that you may be able to bear *it*."

Romans 8:13 (NKJV), "For if you live according to the flesh you will die; but if by the Spirit you put to death the deeds of the body, you will live."

Colossians 3:1-11 (NKJV), "If then you were raised with Christ, seek those things which are above, where Christ is, sitting at the right hand of God. Set your mind on things above, not on things on the earth. For you died, and your life is hidden with Christ in God. When Christ *who is* our life appears, then you also will appear with Him in glory. Therefore, put to death your members which are on the earth: fornication, uncleanness, passion, evil desire, and covetousness, which is idolatry. Because of these things the wrath of God is coming upon the sons of disobedience, in which you yourselves once walked when you lived in them. But now you yourselves are to put off all these: anger, wrath, malice, blasphemy, filthy language out of your mouth. Do not lie to one another, since you have put off the old man with his deeds, and have put on the new *man* who is renewed in knowledge according to the image of Him who created him, where there is neither Greek nor Jew, circumcised nor uncircumcised, barbarian, Scythian, slave *nor* free, but Christ *is* all and in all."

Now here is some advice, wisdom, instruction:

Protect your eye gate. Matthew 6:22-23 "The eye is the lamp of the body. If your eyes are healthy, your whole body will be full of light. But if your eyes are unhealthy, your whole body will be full of darkness. If then the light within you is darkness, how great is that darkness!"

As we discussed in my first book, I had an extreme addiction to pornography; thus, protecting my eye gate is of great importance. I stay away from shows that have any sexual immorality and or nudity. I honestly abhor it. When family members want to watch something that I know has content that I shouldn't watch, I simply leave or go into another room. So, my caution to you is to stay away from certain TV shows. You know yourself better than anyone else. Allow the Holy Spirit to help you identify your dos and don'ts. I still love my action packed, shoot them up type movies, HGTV, renovation, building houses and Animal Planet (smile). But you won't see me watching filth or scary movies.

Protect your ear gate. Watch what you are listening to. Music can open demonic portals in your life. Sounds and frequencies have the ability to open up either demonic or heavenly portals. Certain lustful music can open up doors of sexual perversion in your life; however, worship music can open up heavenly portals. The Bible says faith comes by hearing and hearing the word of God. The opposite is true, if we listen to Satan's lies, worldly music, his false ministers, his accusations, etc. Listening to the wrong thing will affect our hearing gateway. When our hearing gateway is affected, it will make it hard for us to hear the truth of God's word.

Verbal abuse and any other negative speaking can cause blockage to this gate and cause spirits of rejection/spiritual death to enter in. So, what we are listening to is very important. Solomon says in Proverbs 4:24, "stay away from corrupt speech." We need to be quick to avoid people who are always speaking negatively, gossiping, murmuring, or complaining. We need to love, but not spend too much time with people like that because it grieves the spirit of God. Some people are quick when they hear about another child of God who took a fall. They start to talk about that person instead of praying for them. The Bible says in Galatians 6:1-2 [paraphrased], "if any man is overtaken in any trespass, you who are spiritual restore such a one unless it could be you."

Watch your mouth gate (or the tongue). Our words hold power and weight. We are instructed to bridle our tongues though it is a little member it can cause significant damage.

"Death and life are in the power of the tongue," Proverbs 18:21.

Beware of the idle words you speak over yourself and others because we will be judged by every idle word we speak. We must also remember not to use our tongues like curses one minute and blessings the next.

"Can both fresh water and salt water flow from the same spring?" (James 3:11-13).

Proverbs 4:24, "avoid all perverse talk." The more we take charge of our tongues the more we will enjoy the presence of the spirit of God. With these mouths we have, our tongue can be our best friend or our worst enemy.

In Matthew 15:18, Jesus also taught us that our mouth can pollute the soul, "but those things which proceed out of the mouth come from the heart, and they defile a man."

The Lord is saying that if we don't guard the mouth, our words can literally pour spiritual mud on our souls. So, I make a practice to pray Psalms 141:3, "set a guard, o Lord, over my mouth; keep watch over the door of my lips." David was very aware of how wicked the mouth can be. If we speak defiling, critical, abusive, profane words, how can we walk in the spirit.

Paul said to the church of Ephesus in Ephesians 4:29, "let no corrupt word proceed out of your mouth, but what is good for necessary edification, that it may impart grace to the hearers."

Guard also what I like to call your feet gate. Guard where you go. Proverbs 4:26-27, "ponder the path of your feet, and let all your ways be established. Do not turn to the right or the left; remove your foot from evil."

We are born again believers. What does the club or bars have to offer us? It would be nothing but an open door. I know family members and friends invite you to clubs, and places that you know will cause your spiritual journey more harm than good. We need to learn the word, "NO". I love you, but "NO". Yeah, they might say that you're so heavenly minded until you're no earthly good, but don't let the devil deceive you. Just because they straddle the fence doesn't mean you have to. And if God wants you to do evangelism some day at a place you don't normally go, He will make that clear to you.

You must stay away from people who don't want God.

1 Corinthians 15:33, says "Do not be deceived: "Evil company corrupts good habits."

Psalms 1:1-2 says, "Blessed *is* the man Who walks not in the counsel of the ungodly, Nor stands in the path of sinners, Nor sits in the seat of the scornful; But his delight *is* in the law of the LORD, And in His law he meditates day and night."

Don't let people lead you back to your own vomit. Once you go back, it's hard to get back to the place in God where you felt His presence on a regular basis. So, I leave you with these questions.

What are you fixing your eyes on?

What are you listening to?

What is on your playlist in your car?

What have you been speaking with your mouth? Goodness or evil?

Are you going places where you have no business going just to keep up with or impress certain family or friends?

Ok, now, take a breath and let's keep pressing, we are almost there. We must live a spirit-led life to stay free. Romans 8:14 (NIV) says, "For those who are led by the Spirit of God are the children of God." A relationship with the Holy Spirit helps you to sustain your freedom.

Chapter 6
STEPS TO DELIVERANCE

God is a God of deliverance, if you want it, it's yours. God will rescue and set your free from anything that has you bound. Teaching spiritual warfare and deliverance is greatly needed in our churches today. Not only do we need to teach it, but we also individually need to learn self-deliverance.

Am I saying as a new believer, you should be attempting to deliver yourself from something you don't really at this point understand, "no". But, as you grow in God, you will learn how to walk and use the authority He has given you. You can't stay a babe always and calling the Pastor to do everything all the time. Don't get me wrong, you need your Pastor and the Elders of the church; however, as you grow you will see the power of the Holy Spirit as He walks you through some things all on your own.

Mark 16:17-18 says, "And these signs will follow those who believe: In My name they will cast out demons; they will speak with new tongues; they will take up serpents; and if they drink anything deadly, it will by no means hurt them; they will lay hands on the sick, and they will recover."

Remember earlier when I was talking about maintenance and getting your oil changed? Well, I have made it a practice to do self-deliverance. I have written out deliverance prayers for myself and my family and I pray them often. I don't wait until I'm bound up or chained up by the enemy before I take action. Once the enemy is exposed it's too late. Make it a practice.

This ability comes from reading God's word and studying to show yourself approved. Read spiritual warfare books that are spirit-led and full of scripture. Read prayer books that are full of scripture. The Holy Spirit will lead you to the right books to read written by generals of the Lord.

I've read many books that have steps to deliverance. One of my favorites that I will forever recommend is *Pigs in the Parlor* by Frank and Ida Mae Hammond. Frank Hammond, a great general in the Lord, made this statement on page 69, "Usually, a person needs only to learn how to go about self-deliverance. After a person has experienced an initial deliverance at the hands of an experienced minister, he can begin to practice self-deliverance."

You would see that he recommends seven steps to deliverance that is very thorough, I've found that this 3-step process has been effective in my life.

1. Repent: A complete turning away from sin. You must fall out of agreement with anything contrary to the will of God and that had you bound. Repentance

requires you to openly confess all sins, which takes away the legal right of the demon spirit.

2. Renounce: A formal declaration that you have rejected and abandoned sin and it is the action resulting from repentance. This is where you demonstrate that you have truly turned from sin. Example: The night I got saved in 2005, I began to throw away and destroy every object associated with my sins. I had about three big bags full of anything impure, old pictures, jewelry, clothes, bed sheets, comforters, and sex toys. I was making a clean break and fresh start. Therefore, you must destroy all paraphernalia that gives demons a legal right. Your deliverance will be blocked if you hold on to ungodly things. You must renounce and ask God's forgiveness for all involvement in idolatry, the occult, or eastern religions, this includes martial arts and

yoga exercises. Regular stretching is fine; however, doing certain poses and saying ritualistic things will only keep you bound.

Before you enter into step 3, be sure you have the desire to be delivered. You must truly want deliverance, it's kind of crazy, but some people prefer bondage just as there are some homeless people who prefer homelessness. Some people may just like the attention or like to escape into childishness with fear of growing up. There are also some people who would like to keep things in their subconscious mind, like traumas and pains. Demons love to reside in our subconscious. Another way to explain the subconscious is the areas we don't want to deal with. For example: It could be hard or painful to think back on a molestation that occurred, but it needs to be confronted primarily because of forgiveness or guilt.

3. Remove: This is when deliverance starts. According to 1 John 1:9, "If we confess our sins, He is faithful and just to forgive us *our* sins and to cleanse us from all unrighteousness." So, we are making sure we ask for forgiveness for ourselves and that we have forgiven all others. Matthew 6:14-15 says, "For if you forgive men their trespasses, your heavenly Father will also forgive you. But if you do not forgive men their trespasses, neither will your Father forgive your trespasses." Note: Forgiveness is a requirement for your deliverance. The enemy will continue to hold the legal right to stay if you don't forgive those who have wronged you. Then you will pray for God to deliver you and set you free in Jesus's name. This is where knowing God's word and

warfare prayers will be of great use. At this point you know the things that had you bound. Therefore, you will begin to call them out by name in a commanding voice and in faith, ask them to leave in the name of Jesus. Remember, prayer is toward God and warfare is toward the enemy. Luke 10:19 says, "Behold, I give you the authority to trample on serpents and scorpions, and over all the power of the enemy, and nothing shall by any means hurt you." You are now walking in the authority God has given you, so use it like your life depends on it and it does. You are in a spiritual battle for your life.

You would see that these 3 steps incorporate everything that is needed to break free. I leave you also with a prayer for deliverance and a warfare prayer that I wrote during my maintenance, while taking a course in Deliverance Aftercare.

Deliverance Prayer

It is my confession with my mouth and belief in my heart that you died on the cross and rose again on the third day. You did it just for those who believe in you. You loved us so that you gave your only begotten Son, that whosoever believes in you shall not perish but have everlasting life. I love you Lord and I belong to you from this day forward. I ask you to forgive me of all my sins, known and unknown. I renounce them all. I forgive all others who caused me pain or disappointment. Please cleanse me now with your precious blood. I come to you now as Jehovah Mephalti - the Lord my deliverer. You know me better than I know myself. Everything that has had me bound for years. I declare your word that, "Whosoever that calls on the name of the Lord shall be delivered." I call upon you and ask you Lord to deliver and set me free. Satan, I renounce you and all your works, you will no longer keep me bound and I will live the abundant life the Lord came to give me. I come out of agreement and loose myself from you now. I command you and your cohorts to leave right now in Jesus's name! Amen.

Warfare Prayer

Declaration: This will be the best year of my life; I shall have just what I say.

Heavenly Father, holy is your name and greatly to be praised.

I ask the courts of heaven to hear my cry today. I ask the Lord Jesus to be my advocate according to 1 John 2:1-2.

I come to you holy and acceptable according to Romans 12:1.

I exercise my God-given authority in Christ Jesus to judge demons and principalities in the name of Jesus I pray.

I ask you to dismiss all Satan's accusations against me and my bloodline in Jesus's name. I ask you to send angels to destroy every evil altar and execute the Lord's judgement against it.

I uproot the altar of premature death, stagnation, depression, sexual perversion, poverty, witchcraft, pride, retaliation, resentment, procrastination, lack of consistency, anger, unforgiveness, abuse, divorce, infirmity, pride, Jezebel, marine spirits, Delilah spirits, delay, abortion spirits, confusion, lying spirits, fear, trauma, adultery, hopelessness, unfruitfulness, sexual molestation, freemasonry, suicide, laziness, and prayerlessness.

I thank you Lord and I decree and declare that any calamity or misfortune the devil is orchestrating against my life through these evil altars is now cancelled in Jesus's name.

I thank you for the strength to pray and not faint concerning the nation, my family, my church, my relationships, my job, and everything that concerns me.

I decree and declare over my life and health, according to Psalms 103. I thank you for your benefits. I shall live and not die and declare the works of the Lord. I thank you for the strength to pray and to not lose heart, and to not grow weary in welldoing for in due season I shall reap if I faint not.

I decree and declare that everything that the devil stole shall be returned 7-fold. I am prosperous, I am wealthy, I am fearfully and wonderfully made. I am a lender and not a borrower, I am humble and wise. I thank you Lord for the anointing you've placed on my life, and I repent for not walking in it to the fullest. I hereby turn and walk toward you to help accomplish everything you've called me to do. In Jesus's name.

Amen.

Chapter 7
CERTIFICATE OF COMPLETION

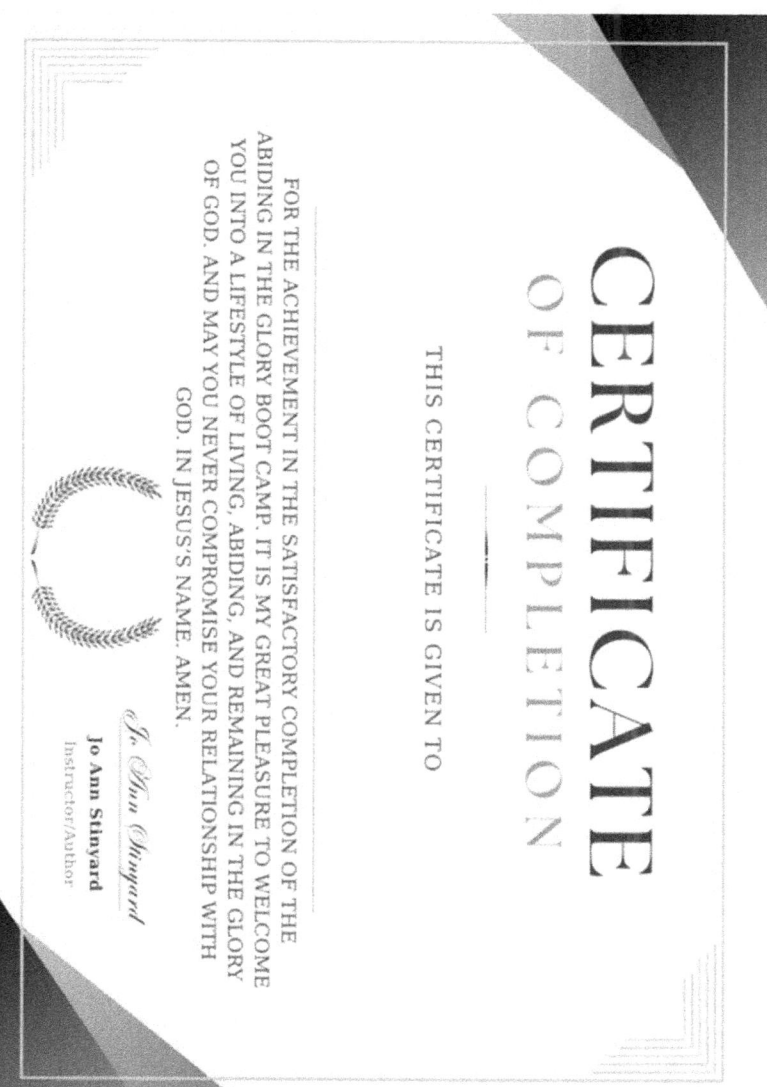

www.ingramcontent.com/pod-product-compliance
Lightning Source LLC
Chambersburg PA
CBHW060423090426
42734CB00011B/2421